PARENTING

# 101

## WAYS TO ROCK YOUR WORLD

Simple strategies for parenting
with sanity and joy

## Susan G. Groner

**Daily Success**
THE BOOK SERIES

Parenting: 101 Ways to Rock Your World

ISBN-13: 9780999476307
ISBN-10: 0999476300

The information and tips in this book are merely suggestions based on the combined knowledge and experience of the authors.

Large quantity purchases of this book are available at a discount. DAILY SUCCESS PUBLISHING books may be ordered through booksellers or by contacting:

DAILY SUCCESS LLC
a division of JFA INC
957 NASA Parkway Suite 101
Houston TX 77058
books@daynasteele.com
(281) 738-3254

Printed in the United States of America
Publish date: October 2017

To my parents, Carol and Morris Gold, and to all the parents that I have learned from and continue to learn from. I use your lessons every day.

—*Sue*

## MORE IN THE 101 WAYS BOOK SERIES

LinkedIn: 101 Ways to Rock Your World

Havana: 101 Ways to Rock Your World

In the Classroom: 101 Ways to Rock Your World

Welcome to College! 101 Ways to Rock Your World

On the Golf Course: 101 Ways to Rock Your World

101 Ways to Rock Your World: Everyday Activities for
Success Every Day

PARENTING

# 101

## WAYS TO ROCK YOUR WORLD

PARENTING: the raising of children and all the responsibilities and activities involved in it.

—Cambridge Dictionary

# In This Book . . .

One of the most frustrating aspects of parenting is that there is no school for it. You learn by doing.

—*Dr. Elliot Barsh, Pediatrician*

# Introduction

## By Elliot Barsh, MD

From the moment we conceive the idea that we can be a parent, long before our first child is conceived, we begin to place expectations on ourselves. We spend much of our time imagining what it will be like, how good we will undoubtedly be at parenting our imaginary children at every imaginable age. Then we have real live children and all of a sudden, it is not as easy to be that "perfect" parent that we imagined ourselves.

One of the most frustrating aspects of parenting is that there is no school for it. You learn by doing. Trial and error. After 29 years as a pediatrician and 18 years as a parent, I have come to understand that feeling like a "good enough parent" is both the key to truly enjoying the journey of parenthood as well as one of the hardest things anyone can try to accomplish.

Our children turn us into parents. If we allow, they can help us expand our ideas about what parenting is and is not.

From the beauty of our newborns' presence, to the joy of our toddlers' and preschoolers' wonder, the self-possessed search for our tweens' identity, and the fast and furious teenaged race towards independence and adulthood, our children depend on us and renew us. Over and over again.

As a parenting mentor, Sue is the guide many of us long for—when we have just said something to our child that we instantly regret, or when we are in uncharted parenting waters, or, most important, when we find ourselves engaging in the same behavior again and again and suffering the same unsatisfying outcomes. In this book, you will find guidance for young children, older children, and everyone in between. You will find yourself more able to make parenting decisions based on long-term goals rather than on in-the-moment or knee-jerk reactions. And, most valuable (in my opinion), you will be reminded to enjoy your time with your children.

Sue Groner's parenting tips provide immediate access to wise and loving guidance that can help when navigating the many day-to-day challenges we encounter when raising children. Her big- picture, common-sense approach offers parents a "tool box" that allows them to act from a position of confidence. Parents will learn the difference between winning battles and winning the war, and that the big, important "win" is always to nurture a child to grow up to be a kind, competent, and independent adult.

With honesty and humor, Sue shares her parenting stories and invites us to join her on this incredible journey. For me, reading her book was like sitting with Sue in my office during one of her children's visits. Thoughtful, practical, and always listening, Sue shares reflections about what she has learned.

Both as a parent and as a professional, I consider *Parenting: 101 Ways to Rock Your World* a great resource for parents at every stage of child-rearing.

ELLIOT BARSH, M.D. is a pediatrician and physician coach in one of New York State's largest medical groups. He also serves as Chief Medical Officer for the North Salem School District and has been named Best Doctor by New York magazine and Westchester Magazine for numerous years. Dr. Barsh, who professes a devotion to family, work, and Batman comics, lives in Somers, New York with his wife Pam and their children Sueann and Jack.

# Opening Words
by Susan G. Groner

When I was a young mother, I was constantly second-guessing my parenting decisions. How much screen time? How much allowance? What type of chores? Music lessons or sports? Scheduled time or downtime? The list was endless.

Friends, articles, and parenting books provided plenty of advice. I would read a chapter or two (who has time to read a whole book?) and embark on a new parenting direction. My husband could always tell when I had embraced a "New Plan" because I would start enforcing new regulations and change how I spoke to the kids. Worst of all, I would become anxious anew that I had been doing everything all wrong. How would my children ever become the smartest, nicest, and most talented kids in the world given that I had messed things up so badly?

What I have come to realize since, is that every child, every parent, and every family unit functions differently and there is no one answer or directive that will work for everyone.

Still, most of us want the same things—for our children to be safe, for our children to feel loved, and for our children to grow up to be confident, capable, caring adults. On top of that,

I wanted to feel good while raising my children. My goal was to find parenting strategies that did not suck the joy out of being a parent.

I have tried many approaches, some with better results than others. One revelation for me was when I decided to let myself become visibly excited about giving my children permission to do something they really wanted to do, rather than behave as if I were reluctantly doing them a big favor. This little shift in attitude helped to make a big difference in my relationship with my kids.

The parenting tips I have culled here are meant to help you relax and find more enjoyment on the route to raising resilient, self-sufficient young adults. This book is designed to be an easy-to-read, pick-up-every-now-and-then reference that may help you look at your parenting style in a different light. If you find a tip that resonates with you, give it a try. If it does not work for you, let it go. Most important, do not get down on yourself if you have been doing things differently. The mere fact that you are reading this book makes you a good parent. It means you are making an effort and that you care.

I am lucky to have been able to continue to learn and grow as a parent from my own mistakes as well as from the mistakes and examples of my dear friends (you know who you are)! I am grateful to my husband, Bill, for his always valuable perspective and endless support. As for my own children, Victoria and Hudson (now 20 and 18), I appreciate having such good-natured test subjects who are always showing me the error of my ways. Among other things, they have taught me that good parenting is a constant learning process and that the true sign of "success" is not that your children are "perfect," but rather that they are happy, capable, and kind.

Books, like children, take a village. I have been fortunate to be able to collaborate with editor Jessica Wolf, who pushed me to be clear and concise, and provided a lot of laughs in the process. And with illustrator Robbie Shilstone, who offered a fresh and modern take on an age-old topic.

Finally, thank-you, Dayna, for encouraging me to write this book in the first place. Like many parents, you do not take enough credit for what a thoughtful, heartfelt job you have done with your own three sons. I hope what I have put together here helps other parents feel more confident, competent, and inspired in discovering what works best for their families.

SUE GRONER is the founder of *The Parenting Mentor,* which provides on-site and virtual coaching sessions for parents of toddlers through teens. As a University of Pennsylvania, Wharton School graduate and a former advertising executive, Groner uses her training in creative problem-solving along with her CLEARR™ methodology to help parents foster and maintain a more fulfilling and stress-free experience while in the trenches of day-to-day childrearing. She lives in New York with her husband and two children.

# Parenting
# Golden Rules

I think Lincoln had a unique
parenting style. He let his kids
run free and wild.

—*Steven Spielberg*

# 1 Say YES with joy

If you know you are ultimately going to drive your child to the mall, let her have a 3-person sleepover or allow an extra cookie after dinner—just go straight to a happy YES! When you offer up an awesome gesture as if you are doing your kids a big favor, it takes the fun out of it. It is so easy to add joy to your delivery with "Sure!" or "I'd be happy to!" or "Let's do that!" Your enthusiasm will make your child feel even better about your YES, but best of all, it will make you feel great.

Your children are not your children.

They are the sons and daughters of Life's

longing for itself.

*—From "On the Children"*
*by Kahlil Gibran*

# 2 Do not brag about your child

When someone brags about how exceptional their child is, do you ever feel, a teeny-tiny bit, as if your child does not measure up? Well, that is how other parents feel when you brag about your child. As parents, we need to keep this tendency in check. Your child may be exceptional, but leave the heralding for the grandparents.

# 3 Respect your team

Teachers, coaches, lesson instructors—they are all a part of your parenting team. Your child may be benched or not performing well at school, and you may be frustrated, but do not yell at or blame someone else. Your child needs to see you treat the authority figures in their lives with respect. Do ask privately and politely if there is something your child could do to thrive more in that environment. Lots can get accomplished through teamwork. Little gets done through finger-pointing or blaming.

# 4 Do not discipline other children

This can get ugly, really fast. Every parent has his or her own way of disciplining, and most are not comfortable with (or appreciative of) someone else taking on that role. Unless the child is in real danger, leave it alone. If a child is being rude in your home or not abiding by your rules, you can simply ask for the child to leave. (Call the parent and explain delicately). You may even want to explain to the child she is welcome back once she can follow the rules of your home. Anything beyond that is just not your place.

# 5 Pay attention to timing, manner, and intonation (TMI)

You know what is likely to set your child off. Do not bring up something stressful the night before an exam, or when he is tired or hungry. Talk about "tough topics" with an "easy" attitude. Keep your word choices neutral, and scrub your vocal inflections clean of any hint of judgment, blame, or negativity. Timing, manner, and intonation can make all the difference in how easily (and willingly) your child is able to engage with you.

Parenthood . . . it's about guiding the next
generation and forgiving the last.

—*Peter Krause*

# 6 Leave your past in the past

When you tell your children, "You do not know how lucky you are . . . ," you are inadvertently burdening them with your old baggage. When a child hears about your past struggles, they take some of that inside themselves. They cannot do anything about your past and they should not feel as though they must. Stories about your own tough fourth-grade teacher are okay as long as they are stories you would share at a dinner party. Anything touchier than that, leave for your own BFFs.

When my kids become wild
and unruly, I use a nice safe playpen.
When they're finished, I climb out.

—*Erma Bombeck*

# 7 Turn off your phone

When you are with your child, set your phone to Do Not Disturb. Or better yet, put it away. This gesture says, "Right now, there is nothing more important than you!" Setting aside time when you can unplug and not be interrupted is essential to quality time with your children. They will know you are with them 100 percent. And as a bonus, you are setting a great example by not being glued to your phone.

The quickest way for a parent to get a child's attention is to sit down and look comfortable.

—*Lane Olinghouse*

# 8 Spend time with people you like

Stop hanging out with people that do not make you feel good about yourself or your parenting. You are not obligated to be friends with or spend time with anyone, even if they are parents of your children's friends. Showing your kids that there is no place in your life for people who bring you down will help your kids learn to navigate their own friendships.

# 9 It is okay to do something for yourself

Whether it's getting a babysitter for an hour or hiring a housekeeper occasionally, we all need assistance sometimes to find some essential alone time. Accept offers of help from friends or family and do not be afraid to ask for what you need. Nap during your child's nap time. Watch mindless television. Take a bath. Call a friend. These short, relaxing snippets of time are not only extremely valuable to your health and well-being, they will help you be a more relaxed parent.

# Family
# Time

Anybody out there who is a parent,
if your kids want to paint their bedroom, as
a favor to me, let them
do it. It'll be OK."

—*From "The Last Lecture"*
*by Randy Pausch*

# 10 Create your own family traditions

You can build "We always . . ." moments around practically anything. "We always wake up to a treasure hunt on our birthdays." "We always play *I Spy* on long car rides." "We always celebrate the last day of school with popsicles in the park." Even if your kids get old enough that they groan when you start performing the Snow Day Dance, deep down they like it. Innocent traditions like these help weave the fabric of family legacy.

# 11 Celebrate family milestones together

Moving into a big girl bed. Learning to ride a bike. Losing a tooth. Getting braces off. You can avoid having one child feel "left out" of another child's "big day" by making it a point to celebrate everyone's milestones as a family. This is an opportunity for siblings to learn to be supportive of one another and enjoy each other's big moments and successes.

# 12 Share your fun childhood stories

Tell your kids about fun facts or happenings from when you were a child, especially stories that correspond to your child's current age. Were you mischievous? Did you forget lines in the school play? Were you a class clown? Did you and your friends have a secret fort in the woods? Kids love to hear these stories. They may ask you to tell them over and over. These stories make you more relatable and sometimes open the door to kids sharing more about their own world. Just remember to leave your negative stories behind.

# 13 Try something new as a family

Is there an activity you have been wanting to try? Cooking a new recipe with some first-time ingredients. Exploring a new town. Maybe you have never been hiking. Now is the time. Have family members take turns at coming up with the ideas. You are sure to have a lot of fun and will create great memories by sharing first-time experiences. You might even invent new family traditions.

## Family Question Ideas:

- What funny thing happened today?
- What one thing did you learn today?
- What act of kindness did you perform today?
- What mistake did you make today?
- What were the three highlights of your day?

# 14 Start meals with a family question

"How was your day?" is a legitimate question but it rarely leads to real conversation and more often shuts it down. Instead, make mealtime sharing fun by creating a set of family questions that keep the conversation flowing. Rotate who gets to ask the question. Encourage new questions and add them to your list. Keep the list handy at meal time.

Childhood is a short season.

—*Helen Hayes*

# 15 Spend alone time with each child

There is no substitute for one-on-one time with each child. Positive, focused attention helps to build and maintain an emotional connection. If you can swing 10 to 15 minutes every day, great. If you cannot, make sure your kids know spending alone time with them is important to you and schedule it whenever possible. To make the most of this time, do whatever your child wants. That might be building a tower or playing make-believe. If your kids are older, maybe ask them to teach you how to play their favorite video game or show you a favorite app.

# 16 Play board games together

Board games are not just fun, they offer opportunities to shake up family roles. Games like *Chutes and Ladders* require luck, not skill, so the littlest family members can win fair and square. Some kids will rule in games like *Pictionary*, *Apples to Apples*, and *Taboo* where being able to anticipate how another player thinks gives you a big advantage. In other words, different board games allow different people's strengths to be rewarded. So, mix up the repertoire and may the best player win.

We've had bad luck with our kids—
they've all grown up.

—*Christopher Morley*

# 17 Schedule a regular call with family members

Weekly calls with your parents and your in-laws is a good place to start. This is not only a great way for your children and their grandparents (aunts, uncles, etc.) to build and maintain close relationships, but it also provides tons of pleasure for Grandma and Grandpa. Nothing beats real visits, but Facetime or Skype calls are second best.

One thing I had learned from watching
chimpanzees with their infants is that having
a child should be fun.

*Jane Goodall*

# 18 Laugh with your kids

There is plenty of science behind the fact that laughing increases bonding hormones and decreases stress hormones. Laughing will not only strengthen your relationships with your children, it may also help them to sleep better and to be more cooperative. And of course, laughing with your spouse can lead to other great things . . .

# 19 Unplug as a family

Spend time together as a family completely unplugged and doing family activities offline. Try a family bike ride, hike, or play hide-and-seek. Have a sing-along, juggle, build a snow-man. Make a batch of popcorn, snuggle up together and read. Turning off phones (and other devices) and stowing them out of sight allows time for focused family fun, relaxation, and interaction. If you can do this regularly, it will become a welcome and enjoyable respite for everyone. Perhaps for you most of all!

# Rules and Respect

If you have never been hated by your child,

you have never been a parent.

—*Bette Davis*

# 20 Say NO with conviction

NO should not be your go-to, knee-jerk response. But when you do say NO, make sure you mean it. If you are not sure, give yourself time to think with a "Let me get back to you on that." Once you deliver your NO, stick to your guns and do not leave the door open for your child's attempts to negotiate. Nicely say, "I have made my decision" and walk away or resume whatever you were doing. There is no need to feel guilty about saying NO. You know what is best for your child. NO does not mean you are being mean. It means you are being a conscientious parent.

# 21 Set boundaries

Family boundaries are personal and individual and arise from asking yourself what you consider non-negotiable. For example, "In this family, we never treat each other with disrespect" is an expectation that stems from your values and a position from which you will not budge. When your child knows that sitting in the front seat of the car before she is old enough is never, ever, ever going to happen, she will come to understand that asking is futile. Knowing where you draw the line helps your child feel safe.

# 22 Set rules

Rules are simply stated guidelines and expectations. They usually refer to behaviors that, when followed, make life run more smoothly. The main reason to have rules is so you do not have to revisit every situation every time it comes up. If your rule is no phones at mealtime, then there is no need to discuss it each time you sit down to eat. Rules are not optional and should be consistently enforced. Unlike boundaries, there are times when rules can be broken, or even reviewed and updated. However, each time you "bend" a rule, you run the risk of diminishing how your child views what is expected of her, so proceed with caution.

Most children threaten at times to run away from home. This is the only thing that keeps some parents going.

—*Phyllis Diller*

# 23 Set limits

Limits are typically for things that can be quantified: bedtime, number of cookies after dinner, hours spent in front of a screen, number of consecutive days a bath can be skipped, etc. You can even set limits on how many times your child can whine on Saturdays. Life is not a free-for-all and limits help (all of us) manage that slippery place between what we want and what is good for us. Setting limits for your child teaches your child how to set limits for himself.

# 24 Let kids help make up the rules

When they are old enough, it is great to have kids participate in the rule-making. When your children are invested in the rules, they will better understand their usefulness and will be more inclined to follow them. Their participation will also help them feel more respected as family members. Allow children to revisit and reevaluate the rules with you as needed. Win, win, win!

# 25 Use an imaginary leash

Have you ever seen one of those extension leashes for dogs? The dog is tethered, but the leash extends (by a lot) to give the dog room to explore. Use this image to offer some independence and freedom to your child. Each year, allow the leash to get a little longer. Maybe they can walk farther with friends, or they can make their own decisions about how to spend birthday money. You can always give the leash a gentle tug if need be. By senior year of high school, your child should be able to function with almost complete independence; the leash should be gone!

Children have never been good at listening to their elders, but they have never failed to imitate them.

—*James Baldwin*

# 26 Speak softly

When you really want your kids to listen, keep your message to a few words and deliver it more quietly than your normal speaking voice. The quieter the voice the bigger the impact.

If your kid needs a role model and you ain't
it, you're both fucked.

—*George Carlin*

# 27 Be consistent

Here is the reason children thrive on consistency: when life is predictable, it makes us feel safe. The best way to end up with dependable kids is for you to model consistency—with rules, with your expectations of them and their responsibilities, and most important, in how you handle your own responsibilities.

# 28 Stoop to their level—literally

When having an important conversation, try to be eye to eye with your children instead of talking to them from above (literally, "talking down to them"). What you say will be heard more openly; they will feel less intimidated. Sit together on the floor and hold your child on your lap, or if you are standing, maybe let your child sit on a counter. If your child is already taller than you, have your discussions sitting down.

Before I got married I had six theories about raising children; now I have six children and no theories.

—*John Wilmot*

# 29 Do nothing

Sometimes it is best to let situations play out on their own. That means: do not interfere, do not get involved, do not engage. If your children are arguing, let them. If they come to you to complain, respond with a simple, "Oh." Your kids will learn to sort things out on their own because they know you are not going to get involved or take sides. Bonus: this will create less sibling rivalry.

# 30 Be a receptive and active listener

When your child is having a bad day, just listen. You do not have to jump in with a solution or life lesson or deliver a speech. All you need to do is be with them the way you would hope your best friend would be with you—with open ears and an open heart. Make it your mission to discover what your child is trying to tell you. Listening is a skill you will get better at the more you do it. Look for facial expressions that may not match what is coming out of her mouth. Then, repeat back in your own words what you think you heard. This lets your child know you are really listening and you think her issues are important. You are also helping your child build better communication skills by modeling yours.

# 31 Respect your child's privacy

Keeping your child safe may sometimes require you to be in their business, but as much as possible, try to run a home where everyone respects each other's physical privacy. When people share a living space, it's important for everyone in the family to feel they have some privacy. Make it a norm for your children to knock on your bedroom door before walking in and for everyone to have privacy in the bathroom. Of course, there are times you will want your kids to keep their bedroom doors open, but it is always nice and respectful to knock.

# 32 Ask kids what they think

Rather than just launching into your own opinions about a problem your child is having with a friend or about a situation at school or even about something going on in your lives together, use probing questions to find out where *she* stands on the issue. Ask: What do you think about what is going on? How do you think this should be handled? What would you do? Remember the active listening tip! Everyone likes to know their opinion is valued and needed.

# Perspective and Judgment

# 33 Do not cry (or yell) over spilled milk

Accidents happen. If your child knocks over a glass of milk while you're frantically trying to get dinner on the table, it may seem like a big deal, but it's not. Keep things light—"Oh, don't you hate when that happens?"—and throw him a towel so he can wipe it up. Children falter as do adults. They get paint on their favorite pants. They lose their most cherished toy—again. Don't harp on every little mishap. Your child already feels bad enough about those things. Practice cutting your child a break. Not only will this create a happier home, but your accepting attitude will teach him to cut himself (and others) a break when the millions of silly little things that go wrong in life inevitably pop up.

You can learn many things from children.
How much patience you have, for instance.

—*Franklin P. Adams*

# 34 Do not compare

Some children are organized. Some children love to read. Some children like having lots of friends. Some children eat anything you put in front of them. Every child has strengths. And, every child has weaknesses. Comparing your child to another, whether it is their friend, their brother, or the son of your high school bestie, does not make them feel good. If you believe your child is falling short in bedroom tidiness, approach the topic directly—talk about *their* toys on the floor and *their* unmade bed—rather than making them feel like they are not as good as someone else.

# 35 Embrace boredom

When your child is bored, it does not mean you need to drop whatever you're doing to entertain her. This is a short-term solution that serves only to let your child know that boredom needs to be fixed and you are the one who will fix it. Explain not every moment of every day is scintillating. Remind them they have the best tool to make anything more interesting: their own imagination. When you help your child learn how to find (or make) their own fun, they get to have a life where routine or tedious experiences (like doing laundry or waiting in line) are not things to dread, and can even be brain-freeing moments to look forward to.

# 36 Do not worry about their college until high school

Your child will probably get into college even if she has not become the best violin player in your time zone by second grade. You will meet parents that try to convince you otherwise, but only because someone already convinced them. Childhood and adolescence are times to try different things and discover what you like. Most kids who are groomed for college through some activity end up hating it by the time they apply. College is just another period in your child's life; it is not the end game. If college does not fit into your child's plans, support the decision to attend a trade school, acquire a specialized certification, or pursue anything else she might need to follow her dreams and passions.

# 37 Have realistic expectations

If you expect things to be perfect, you will undoubtedly be disappointed—often. If you expect that things will sometimes go wrong, you can relax and laugh about it when they do. Planning your child's birthday party? Arranging a special evening with your partner? Looking forward to a family afternoon? Enjoy the planning and the process but do not *expect* a flawless event. Adjusting expectations helps you go with the flow.

Having children is like living in a
frat house—nobody sleeps,
everything's broken, and there's a
lot of throwing up.

—*Ray Romano*

# 38 Your child is not a Mini-Me

This may come as a shocker, but your child is going to like things you do not like and may be interested in things you are not interested in. Just because you loved playing piano, doesn't mean she will. She may love dancing even if you have two left feet. Rather than directing your children toward your interests and talents and thereby discounting their own dreams and passions, offer them opportunities to discover what *they* love. Don't worry. There will be plenty of other ways your little apple falls close to the tree.

It is amazing how quickly the kids learn to drive a car, yet are unable to understand the lawnmower, snowblower or vacuum cleaner.

—*Ben Bergor*

# 39 Lose the P word

Move away from "Perfect" in all its forms: perfectly ... perfected ... perfection. Striving for perfection can create unnecessary stress for you and your children. It also causes disappointment as it is usually an unobtainable goal. Kids often avoid trying something new because they don't think they will be successful. So instead of evaluating the result, praise for hard work and effort. Similarly, you do not have to be a Super Mom to be a great mom. Rather than judging yourself against a Perfect ideal, praise yourself for what you have done and start to embrace the delicious feeling of being "good enough."

A two-year-old is like having a blender, but you don't have a top for it.

—*Jerry Seinfeld*

# 40 Failure is your friend

Every chance you get, let your child know failure is a merely one step in the learning process. Let him know frustration is not only normal but a necessary part of mastering something new. Let him see you struggle to learn something. Likely, your child sees you doing only what you are already good at. Share with him out loud what you think you might do differently next time you attempt that pineapple upside-down cake. And, ask him what he might do differently if he is having trouble landing that kick flip. There is no such thing as failure if you learn something from it moving forward.

# 41 Call your childhood self to mind

Try to remember what you were like as a child or teen. Be honest. Were you the super- organized person you are today? Did you do everything you were told? Were you the perfect specimen of a child; after you they broke the mold? Chances are, the answer to each of these questions is no. It takes a long time for the rational, good-sense, non-impulsive part of our brains to develop fully; estimates are 25 years! Children are evolving into the grown-ups they will eventually become— just as you did. Keep that in mind.

# 42 Everyone is different

This seems obvious, but it is worth reminding yourself you and your child are not necessarily wired the same way. She may not be organized by nature. He may not be a morning person. You may be a procrastinator and have a child who gets stressed out when she is not on time. We all march to the beat of our own drums, and when you parent to their beat, rather than the beat you think they *should* be playing, you and your child can develop a lovely rhythm together.

Having children is like having a bowling alley installed in your brain.

—*Martin Mull*

# 43 Do not pick or judge your children's friends

At some point, your child will have a friend or two (or three) who you just do not care for. A tough guy, a queen bee, a kid with no manners, a youngster who is not as studious as you would like. Resist the urge to "shield" your child, and keep your negative opinions to yourself. A friend that does not fit your child's usual mold may fill a need you are not aware of. Maybe she needs a break from feeling like such an academic or she wants to try and fit in more with the cool kids. Maybe this friendship is an opportunity for her to learn how to put on a little makeup or master a video game. Let your child learn to feel confident maneuvering the ups and downs of friends and cliques on her own.

Parenting is not for sissies. You have to sacrifice and grow up.

—*Jillian Michaels*

# 44 Pick your battles

Not everything is worth an argument. If your child wants to
hang posters in her room but you do not think they go with
the décor or you do not want to ruin the walls or you simply
do not like them, first ask yourself: Is my child going to get
hurt by doing this? Is *anyone* going to get hurt? Is this really
a big deal in the grand scheme of things? This brief line of
questioning can be employed for clothing choices, food
choices, movie choices—practically anything. Your ability to
not sweat the small stuff will not only keep the peace, it also
helps your child understand the importance of things you *do*
need to clamp down on.

# 45 Adjust your attitude about mistakes

Telling your child to learn from her mistakes is a great lesson—one of the most important—but you need to walk the walk. Shifting your own idea about mistakes or problems changes your worldview. What if you taught your children to welcome their mistakes, to try and find them, rather than live life trying to avoid them? What if you sat down at dinner and said, "What mistakes did we each make today?" What if everyone in your family felt they could share mishaps without feeling judged? You can almost hear the sighs of relief.

# 46 Do not dismiss your children's concerns

Kids' concerns can seem random and outlandish; your job is to figure out what they are really asking. "Mommy, what if you get really sick?" probably means "Who is going to take care of me?" Telling her that her concern is ridiculous and you are never going to be that sick does not make her feel safe. Children feel anxious about a lot of things they do not yet know how to put into words. Concrete information can quell that anxiety. "If I ever get really sick, Aunt Tilly will come to stay." Children always feel better if they know you have things under control or have a plan.

# 47 Ignore the judgy parents

Parent opinions vary widely on how to raise children: how kids should dress, which movies they should be able to watch, how much screen time they should be allowed, what they should eat, how they are disciplined in public. The list is endless and exhausting. One day, you will get "the look" from another parent (or a group of parents). Remind yourself that your job is not to raise your child based on someone else's opinions or methods. Be clear about your own values and ignore the rest.

Education, like neurosis, begins
at home.

—*Milton Saperstein*

# 48 Don't you be judgy either

If you might accidentally be *that* parent, try and remember that most parents are doing the very best they can. If you believe you have helpful, non-judgmental advice that can be delivered in a non-offensive way—in other words, kindly and with understanding—try it once and see how it goes. If the parent bristles or seems put off, feel free to step away from your Perfect Parent Mission and join the rest of us down here in the trenches.

The child supplies the power but the parents
have to do the steering.

—*Benjamin Spock*

# 49 Monitor praise

Children need an internal voice that lets them know how capable they are. The way they develop that is not by being told repeatedly and excessively they are the best thing that has ever happened to humanity. Use your child's accomplishments to engage her in developing her own internal voice. Instead of, "You are such an amazing Lego builder," how about, "You must feel very proud of what you've built!" As much as possible, avoid phrases like, "You are soooo beautiful!" "You are the BEST..." "You are incredible!" "You are sooo talented!" You want to build your child's self-esteem from the inside out, not the outside in.

# Gratitude and Attitude

Never lend your car to anyone to whom you
have given birth.

—*Erma Bombeck*

# 50 Do not over-indulge

Overdoing it with toys, clothes, and gifts creates long-term problems. It sets an expectation in our children that they should be showered with "stuff" all the time. In addition to fostering a mindset of instant gratification, it creates children who grow up with a sense of entitlement. Ask yourself why you feel the need to give, give, give. When a child has time to dream about something she wants and must also learn to wait for that thing, it sets the groundwork for lifelong motivation and coping skills. Provide for your children based on your vision of the adults you hope they become.

# 51 Practice empathy

Sympathy is when you feel sorry for someone; it usually leaves the person feeling like a victim. Empathy is when you let someone know you understand, and it leaves them feeling less alone with their troubles. Your 5-year-old is upset because he got a chocolate cupcake rather than a vanilla cupcake at a birthday party. You do not have to fix things; you simply need to validate them. "Oh sweetie, I can see you are really disappointed. I would feel sad too if I didn't get my favorite flavor." Try empathy when your fifth grader does not get the teacher she wants, or your teen cannot wear his favorite jeans because they are in the laundry. Empathy is an emotion diffuser and a relationship builder.

# 52 Talk about gift-getting

If half your life is spent on picking up, sorting, and storing toys, your child may have enough of them. Before the birthday party invitations go out, assess with her whether she would like to do gifts differently this time. Some gifts can be donated to a homeless shelter. Or she can tell party guests she's raising money for your local charity and ask them to bring a donation ($7 for a 7-year-old!). Do not force your child to forego the gifts, but offer her the opportunity to experience how giving can be 100 times more satisfying than receiving.

Don't worry that children never listen to you; worry that they are always watching you.

—*Robert Fulghum*

# 53 Engage in family service projects

Doing service as a family creates connection and closeness. It feels good to help other people and it feels good to grow up in a family that does it together. Aside from instilling social consciousness and providing for those in need, service work opens your child's heart in a way few other things can. Find a local community organization to support. Engage children in the discovery. You can serve meals at a shelter or descend on an elderly neighbor's weedy lawn. There is no shortage of ways to help. And, there are no limits to the benefits of offering service.

Every day of our lives we make deposits in
the memory banks of our children.

—*Charles R. Swindoll*

# 54 Schedule family donation time

Set aside a few times throughout the year, perhaps at the end of each season, to gather old clothes, linens, toys, and any other items you want to discard, and donate the gently-used items to a local charity. Each family member should find at least a few items of their own to contribute. This is a good way to clean out closets, drawers, toy chests, garages, cabinets, everything! Clothes that are no longer worn, toys no longer played with, items with missing lids—get rid of them. Sometimes you even find things you were looking for or things you forgot you had.

The interesting thing about being
a mother is that everyone wants pets, but no
one but me cleans the
kitty litter.

—*Meryl Streep*

# 55 Replace chores with contributions

One easy way to make chores not seem like such a chore is to stop calling them that. Instead, they become family contributions. Teach your 2-year-old to collect dirty clothes into a basket. Have your 7-year-old water the plants. Explain to the kids that you are all on the same team working for household success. Be a cheerleader rather than a drill sergeant. When kids are pitching in—no matter what size the contribution—life skills are learned, families grow closer, and it is another inoculation against the entitlement epidemic.

# 56 Smile big and often

Smiling is not only a result of happiness, some research suggests it may also be the cause. When you smile, you are apt to be less stressed, less bothered by what is going on around you, and probably more likely to be heard by your child. Your tone changes when you are smiling; your child can hear the difference and it sets the tone for the energy in your home. Smiling is easy, free, and infectious. Go ahead. Make your day!

# 57 Teach and model gratitude

Studies show people who feel gratitude are less depressed, better able to handle stress, and more optimistic. Tell your children what you feel grateful for. Regularly. Do not just leave this for Thanksgiving. Some days it may just be gratitude for whoever invented mint toothpaste or chocolate. An attitude of gratitude lets your child go through life looking for what is awesome. How awesome is that?

# 58 Practice random acts of kindness together

Look for opportunities to perform random acts of kindness in front of your kids and encourage them to do the same. Help someone cross the street, hold open a door, say something nice to a stranger. Without making it too big a deal, talk about what it felt like to do something nice and unexpected. Talk about what they imagine the other person felt like. And, if someone holds a door open for you, take a moment to mention how it made you feel. "I love when that happens!" sends a loud and clear message to kids how easy it is to be kind and how much it is appreciated.

# Food and Dining

At every step the child should be allowed to meet the real experience of life; the thorns should never be plucked from his roses.

—*Ellen Key*

# 59 Let kids order their own meals

Telling a waitperson what he would like to have for dinner allows your child to practice many skills: speaking to grown-ups they do not know, using please and thank you, advocating on their own behalf, maintaining eye contact, asking questions if they are unsure about something. Restaurants are a safe, low pressure environment where you can easily come to the rescue in a face-saving manner if things go awry.

# 60 Branch out from the kids' menu

Use restaurant meals to help your child develop a taste for new foods. If he insists on the mac and cheese from the kids' menu, make a rule he needs to taste something from the grown-up menu too. If your child does not care for something, ask her why. It might be the texture, or the sauce, or something entirely different. Let kids know there are lots of options beyond chicken fingers.

# 61 Keep Oreos around

Kids like to be places where there are good snacks. Having something fun to nibble on is a way of making your kids' friends feel welcome. If you are a family that does not typically do cookies or junk food, keep a guest stash of snacking options that will not make eyes roll. Not everyone wants to nibble on quinoa squares. Crazy, but true.

The most remarkable thing about my mother is that for thirty years she served the family nothing but leftovers. The original meal has never been found."

—*Calvin Trillin*

# 62 Have kids prepare their own meals

Spreading peanut butter on bread, pouring a bowl of cereal, or rinsing off an apple are good for starters and make your kids feel capable. Having a repertoire that includes more than ripping open a bag of chips gives them more freedom and independence (and healthy choices) around after-school snacks. It is never too early for a child to start learning his way around food. Plus, the more competent your child is in the kitchen, the more appetizing breakfast in bed will be on your birthday!

# 63 Avoid turning food into a control issue

If your child refuses to eat a meal, you do not need to make her eat. She will eat at the next meal. Skipping a meal is no big deal. If she is hungry, let her make a peanut butter and jelly sandwich for herself. For young children, this is one of the few areas where they have control. Power struggles around food and eating are something you want to avoid. Try and keep meals about connecting as a family; do not make food and mealtime a war zone.

# 64 Be a role model with your own eating habits

If you do not want your kids to eat standing at the counter or picking the crumbs off the coffee cake, do not let them see you do it. Ditto if you do not want them to eat the exact same thing for every single meal. Overeating, under-eating, picky eating, speed eating—they are going to learn a lot from you. What sort of food role model are you?

Tell me and I forget, teach me and I may remember, involve me and I learn.

—*Benjamin Franklin*

# 65 Have family dinner often

Family dinners are linked to everything from higher self-esteem to lower incidences of substance abuse. If you or your partner work too late to make this realistic, maybe try a family milk and cookies before bedtime. Or a family breakfast a few times a week. Coming together regularly, all of you, sets family time as an important commitment. Even if it seems inconvenient, kids grow to value this stabilizing ritual in their lives.

# 66 Have kids participate in meal prep and clean-up

Peeling carrots. Setting the table. Pouring water. Clearing dishes. Filling the dishwasher. There is practically no end to what your child can help you with. It does not need to be a big something, but it should be a regular something. Teach your child early that meals do not just happen and many hands make light work. Helping allows kids of all ages to feel useful and important. It also teaches kids that being helpful is awesome.

Indeed—judicious, consistent parenting is a dream of mine. No judgments, learning space and listening carefully are my goals.

—*Emma Thompson*

# 67 Use the 80/20 rule

Do not create a life of stress around food. Eighty percent of the time, try to eat healthy foods, organic when you can, avoiding excessive sugar and carbs. The other 20% of the time, relax and enjoy. The stress of trying to eat only organic, grass-fed, whole-grain, unprocessed, extra-virgin everything can be worse for your health than occasionally eating food that is not ideal. This rule of thumb will also help older children navigate the junk food wasteland when you are not around.

Perhaps it takes courage to raise children.

—*John Steinbeck*

# 68 Sometimes break the rules

Breaking food rules not only makes you seem more fun, it also helps kids understand diets that are too restrictive are not what life is about. Offer ice-cream for breakfast or pancakes for dinner. Let them pick whatever unconventional meal they want on their birthday or packed for their school lunch! Have a no-veggie vacation! Breaking food rules on occasion is silly and fun, and nobody will get hurt. Your children will think this is the greatest thing ever.

# Forbidden
# Phrases

# 69 What did you do in school today?

After a full day of school and other activities, your children may want to chill by themselves to unwind, download, or regroup. Most kids need to decompress when they get home. Leave them alone and do not start asking about their day until dinnertime. Instead, tell them about your day. If they're getting in the car, play some music they like. When they come off the school bus, have a snack waiting. These little acts show love.

# 70 Leave me alone

When your child wants to spend time with you, hearing you say, "leave me alone" can feel hurtful. Even adults do not want to hear this from anyone. If you need to be alone, explain this to your child; tell her when you will be available and how you look forward to spending time with her. If your child does not yet tell time, keep a little kitchen timer on hand, set it and ask her to come get you when it goes off. If you need to be alone because you are exhausted and need some me-time, explain this too. They may be kids but they will understand you are human. This is another excellent time to model communication skills and how people need to take care of themselves.

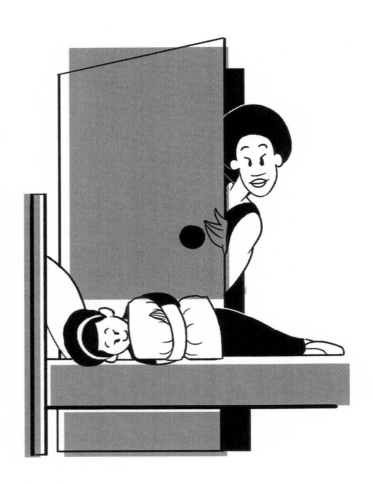

# 71 Go to your room

This will make your child feel alone and unloved at a time when they need your love and support. Your reason for sending your child away is most likely because of some sort of acting up or bad behavior. Let your child know you recognize they are angry, frustrated, or sad, and then hold them tight. If this does not work, tell your child you are going to give them a little time in their room to let out their frustrations. Check in a few minutes later and give more hugs.

Don't try to make children grow up to be like you, or they may do it.

—*Russell Baker*

# 72 What were you thinking?

Or "Why would you do that?" or "What is the matter with you?" serve only to belittle your child and make her feel terrible about herself. Chances are she was not really thinking at all. When your children make mistakes or do things they should not have done, instead of accusing or yelling, ask them what they might have done differently. Give them time to reflect; they may not figure things out right away. Asking this question gives them an opportunity to problem solve and to revisit a poor choice without making them feel any worse than they already do.

It's not what you do for your children,
but what you have taught them to do for
themselves, that will make them successful
human beings.

—*Ann Landers*

# 73 Wow, that is great!

When your child shows you their latest masterpiece, responding with, "That's beautiful" or, "I love it!" is certainly positive, but it does not convey your engagement. In fact, in some cases, it can even make you seem uninterested or dismissive, surely the opposite of what you hope to communicate. Instead try, "Tell me about this piece of art!" Be specific with your compliments: "I love your use of colors!" Pointing out details in his work—from art projects to term papers—helps build your child's self-esteem.

# 74 You are a bad child

Avoid labeling. Telling your child she is "bad" because she hit her brother is a message that may stay with her long after the incident has passed. It may even unintentionally become part of how she sees herself—which is probably not what you want! If you must label, keep it to the behavior, not the person. Say "Hitting is bad" rather than "You are bad".

# 75 Why didn't you ... ?

No matter how you fill in the blanks, this question will sound judgmental and will put your child on the defensive. Instead, try helping him come up with a better way to remember a responsibility or whatever was forgotten. Again, this helps children learn to problem solve now and throughout their lives.

It is easier to build strong children than to repair broken men.

—*Frederick Douglass*

# 76 Lose the word *stupid*

This is one instance where, even if you are talking about a be-havior, your child is going to hear and think *she* is stupid. Any way you use it, it's insulting. And if your child did do some-thing really stupid, chances are she already knows it. Choose your words carefully; use your best judgment to decide how you will not sound judgmental.

I know how to do anything.

I'm a mom.

—*Roseanne Barr*

# 77 Go ask your (other parent)

Without the proper context, sending your child to a different parent can come across as a lack of interest or as dismissive. Here are some alternatives: "I don't know how to do that but I think Dad might know." "I am in the middle of something but Mom might be available. If not, I am happy to help when I am done." If your child is asking for permission, tell him you're not sure yet and you'll discuss it with Dad. This allows you and your partner to be on the same page without your child feeling pawned off on the other parent.

# Life
# Skills

What separates privilege from entitlement
is gratitude.

—*Brené Brown*

# 78 Write thank you notes

Someday, when the US Post Office becomes obsolete, snail mail thank you notes can be dispensed with, but even then, something equally as thoughtful and personal should take their place. Let children know hand-written notes are treasures. When anyone bestows a kindness—a gift or even just a great time—putting some extra effort into conveying appreciation is a simple way to make someone feel good.

# 79 Teach your kids to use an alarm clock

It is not your job to wake your children. It is merely your job to provide them with the tools they can use to wake up on their own. Start young and let your child know he is such a big boy, you bet he can use an alarm clock. This is a very easy way to give children some power and control over their lives. Older kids can use the alarm feature on their phones. And, very young children can be taught they cannot wake you up until the alarm goes off—an extra treat for you!

# 80 Teach your kids to hydrate

Got a headache? Drink water. Feeling tired? Drink water. Hungry even though you just ate? Drink some more water. A glass of water first thing in the morning is a great habit to instill in kids. Don't wait until thirst sets in. Few of us drink enough water, and when we are not sufficiently hydrated, nothing in our body works as well as it could or should. This old saying holds true: your wee should be clear, not yellow!

# 81 Be on time

If you can learn to be on time, your kids will learn to be on time as well. If you are rushing around at the last minute, yelling for your kids to pack up and get in the car, this will be their normal. Set the example and then make sure your kids are on time for school, practice, lessons, doctor appointments, everything. Prepare in advance, build in extra travel time, and keep away from your phone. When you stop to check your email one more time, before you know it, you are late. Set a good example.

# 82 Remember the importance of sleep

Not only do you need to be well-rested, but your children need plenty of sleep as well. Lack of sleep makes for cranky, irritable children. In addition, they will be less engaged and less focused at school and less able to handle little stressors. Good sleep habits are touted as a cornerstone in the lives of many successful people, so get your kids started on this early.

# 83 Model patience

Children are not born patient. They learn to be patient, and they learn it from watching you. So, when you are in a slow line at the store or in stand-still traffic on the way to the water park, take a deep breath before you start your rant. Show your child that it is okay to be frustrated by something and still have a sense of humor about it. This will make everyone's life better.

# 84 Teach your kids how to do their own laundry

Separating lights and darks, measuring the soap, and using the buttons and dials on the washing machine and dryer are all easy ways a young child can pitch in with this never-ending chore. Slightly older children can match socks. By middle school, your child should be able to do their own laundry from amassing, to folding, to putting it away. Does that mean they *must* do their laundry? That is up to you.

Parenting is an impossible job

at any age.

—*Harrison Ford*

# 85 Skills instead of solutions

Have you ever solved a problem, big or small, and walked away feeling proud? That is the same feeling a child gets every time they conquer something in their world. It makes them more competent, capable, and confident. Every time you solve a problem for your child, you rob them of one of those experiences. Break down and coach the skills needed to solve a problem. If something seems irreparable, ask, "What do you think you (or we) should do next time?" Ask, don't tell. This is mentoring, not fixing.

The best way to keep children at home is to make the home atmosphere pleasant, and let the air out of the tires.

—*Dorothy Parker*

# 86 Teach kids to advocate for themselves

Coach your child in the skills required to get what they need in the world. This can start with having them ask to borrow another child's shovel at the beach and evolve into encouraging them to talk to teachers, coaches, store clerks, and other parents. Role play early on so they feel comfortable. When children can advocate for themselves, they can create situations in which they can thrive. Each time they do, they become better and more comfortable at it.

# 87 Teach OHIO— Only Handle It Once

A dirty plate skips the sink and goes right in the dishwasher. A coat comes off, skips the living room chair, and goes straight to a hook or hanger. Open a box, put the contents away, and toss the box in the garbage. Having a fun way to remind your child (and everyone in the house) of a rule or life skill makes it sound less like nagging and more like a secret code. Putting things away begins with knowing where things go. Remember, a place for everything and everything in its place. And, sometimes that place is in the trash.

# 88 Foster independent travelers

Just as you taught them to order food for themselves and do their own laundry, you can help your children become competent, savvy travelers. Sit with your young children and make a list of what they want to bring on family trips. As they get older, let them pack for themselves. If you're adventurous, you can even assign parts of your vacation itinerary to your kids. When they're in college and need to book a train ticket home, they will have the confidence to do so.

# 89 Teach money skills

Your child needs to learn how to manage money. Allowance is not payment for services (chores), it is money you *allow* your child to have, simply for being a family member. If your child has a weekly income, you can teach her how to save for something she wants. She will learn how to valuate toys, candy, make-up, or arcade games. You can guide at first, but try not to judge how allowance is spent. Let her make her mistakes and learn her lessons here and now, rather than years from now with credit cards.

# 90 Not all feelings are good, and that is okay

Sometimes our children are not happy and, as parents, we often feel the urge to "fix" that. While our instincts drive us to step in, it is important for kids to develop coping skills. It *is* tough when your child is excluded from a party, does not get a part in the play, or is benched during a game. Be there to acknowledge their feelings and give them a hug, but stay away from interfering phone calls or emails. Once we see our kids can handle *unhappy* on their own, our anxiety will dissipate and we will not feel the need to make everything better.

# 91 Teach a proper handshake

First impressions matter, and being able to execute a proper handshake will set your child up for making a good one. Whether you're going to a new doctor or meeting the parents of new friends, this is a skill to have in the bag. A good handshake consists of three simple elements:

A firm (not crushing) grip.

Looking the person in the eye.

Saying, "Nice to meet you."

Practice at home. Children of all ages should be able to execute a good handshake.

# 92 Teach good table manners

Good table manners can start with a YouTube video on how to use a fork and knife properly. Then, there are a few simple rules you can teach your child so they will always feel comfortable at any table:

Put your napkin on your lap

Wait to eat until everyone is served

Compliment the cook

Help clear the table

Bonus points: never sit until the cook is seated.

The apple never falls far from the tree.

—*Traditional proverb*

# 93 Coach *please* and *thank you*

This may seem obvious, but unfortunately it is not. "Please" and "thank you" can never be said too much. Mastering this simple social skill will put your kids in good stead for their entire lives. Coach them until it is deeply ingrained. Set a good example by thanking parents after a playdate; thank the person who makes dinner; thank the waitress at the diner; thank the bus driver. Please, keep reminding your kids, and thank them as well.

# Family
# Management

My mother's menu consisted of two
choices—take it or leave it.

—*Buddy Hackett*

# 94 Have a grab-and-go option for breakfast

As your kids get older, they will be less likely to want to sit down for breakfast before school. Having something nutritious around that they can take to eat on the bus or as a snack in school may be more realistic and will help keep the peace first thing in the morning. Protein bars, yogurt, fruit and cheese, and trail mix are some ideas. Put these items on your grocery list and pre-make something like pumpkin muffins or hard-boiled eggs over the weekend so they are ready to go first thing Monday morning.

# 95 Pack the night before

Pack up whatever you need the night before—and have your children do the same. Homework, musical instrument, sports attire and equipment, snacks, whatever they need to succeed the next day. Think how much more relaxed mornings will be if the backpacks and all the extras are by the door and ready to go. No more scrambling for that missing cleat or the music for after-school band practice. Even if your kids come home before after-school activities, have them pack everything up the night before. Bonus – you will avoid being late!

# 96 Create routines

Just as we love traditions, most of us love routines, and kids thrive on them. Critical times tend to be in the morning before school and at bedtime. Allowing your kids to be part of establishing the routines will make them more likely to be willing participants. Do they want to make their bed or get dressed first? Put on pajamas or brush their teeth first? Make a chart together (adding pictures for your little ones) and hang it up. Then, stick to it.

# 97 Create a dressing system

Fighting with your kids about what they should wear is no fun at all. Try giving your children some control over their attire by creating three different categories:

Wear anything

Nice casual

Dressy

Once your child knows which clothes fit into each category, let them select for themselves. You'll avoid arguments and be teaching them it is important to dress appropriately for different occasions.

# 98 Make dinner plans

Take some stress out of mealtimes by minimizing how often you need to ask yourself what you're going to make for dinner. Keep a list of successful meals and rotate through them. You can also relegate a certain dish or type of dish to a day of the week, such as Meatless Mondays or Taco Tuesdays. Maybe there is one day each week where you serve something completely new like Trying Fridays. Let the kids be involved in this plan as well.

# 99 Archive electronically

Store your child's creations electronically. You can include every piece of art or only the ones you both love. You can include every gold-starred homework sheet or just the Mother's Day poems. Apps are available for just this purpose, probably developed by parents who either suffered extreme guilt about throwing away anything sentimental or did not have enough closet space for the myriad plastic bins needed to contain a lifetime of Cheerio art.

Our most treasured family heirlooms are our sweet family memories. The past is never dead, it is not even past.

—*William Faulkner*

# 100 Create a notebook to organize milestone materials

Make each of your children a loose-leaf notebook with file folders for each grade. Include their annual doctor's report, school and team photos, report cards and any special certificates. When your child is done with high school, you will have documentation of all the important records. And, when they move into their own place, it makes a fun gift to pass on.

# One Last Tip

# 101 Love 'em every chance you get

Before you know it, they will be grown and starting their own lives. Grab that hug at every opportunity. In fact, try not to leave the house without a hug, a kiss, or an "I love you." It's unlikely you will ever regret making this effort, no matter how pressed you are for time. You will always be your child's parent, but your time together really does go fast.

If it's not one thing, it's your mother.

—*Pillow in Dayna's house*

# Final Words

## By Dayna Steele

There are three things about me that always surprise people—I am a closet gourmet chef, I am a technology geek, and I have always wanted to be a mom as far back as I can remember. Always.

I often tell people I knew I wanted to marry Charlie, aka Wonder Husband, the minute I laid eyes on him. That is true, but I think the full confirmation came at the Houston airport after we had been dating for about six months. I was living in Los Angeles and flying back and forth as often as possible to see Charlie. Many times, it was his weekend to have his very young son, Cris, from his first marriage.

One trip back, when you could still walk your friends and family all the way to the gate, my two men were seeing me back to California. As I walked down the jetway after kisses and hugs, Cris broke away from Charlie and came running after me. He threw his little 2-year-old arms around my legs, looked up with those beautiful blue eyes and said, "Mimi (his nickname for me), please don't go. I love you."

As I settled in my seat, I knew it was going to be only a

matter of time before I moved back to Houston to become wife to Charlie and bonus mom to Cris. Dack followed a few years later, and then Nick. I know I did not follow all the tips in this book all these years, and there are several I probably should have. With that said, all three have grown into fine men like their father, and they are everything I ever imagined and more.

Even though it is something I have always wanted to do, parenting has also been the most difficult thing I have ever tried to master. And you know what? I do not think you ever actually do. Again, nothing and no one is perfect. However, Sue Groner is about as close as you can get to the ideal mom. In fact, she often reminds me of my own mom who was an amazing role model. When Sue mentioned doing a parenting book, I could not strap her to a desk fast enough to get her started. Her tips are that P word we are not supposed to use.

You will find contact information for Sue and me at the end of this book. Never hesitate to reach out if you have questions, need help or even have suggestions for a possible Volume Two. Parenting takes a village—a really, really, big village!

To this day, it is always interesting to me how many people are surprised I am a mom *and* a pretty good one at that (if I may say so myself).

Yes, I am and I am still loving every minute of it! Now, where are those grandkids I need?

DAYNA STEELE is the creator of the *101 Ways to Rock Your World* book series as well as a popular business speaker and storyteller. She is the mother of two sons and the stepmother to a bonus son and daughter-in-law. Dayna is also a rock radio Hall of Famer and the author of *Surviving Alzheimer's with Friends, Facebook, and a Really Big Glass of Wine.*

## OTHER BOOKS BY DAYNA STEELE

Surviving Alzheimer's with Friends, Facebook, and
a Really Big Glass of Wine

Rock to the Top: What I Learned about Success
from the World's Greatest Rock Stars

# Contact Information

SUSAN G. GRONER
sue@theparentingmentor.com
www.TheParentingMentor.com
(914) 522-3763
Instagram: @theparentingmentor
Twitter: @parentmentoring
Facebook: The Parenting Mentor


DAYNA STEELE
dayna@daynasteele.com
www.DaynaSteele.com
(281)738-3254
Instagram: @daynasteele
Twitter: @daynasteele
Facebook: Dayna Steele

Loving a child doesn't mean giving in to all his whims; to love him is to bring out the best in him, to teach him to love what is difficult.

—*Nadia Boulanger*

# About The Illustrator

Robbie Shilstone is an illustrator and animator specializing in hand-drawn cel animation. His works range from comical and whimsical, to dynamic and engaging. Whether through animation or illustration, he tells stories throughout his work. Robbie is currently working on a children's book aimed to raise awareness about climate change. For more of his work go to his website: shilstonearts.com.

NOTES:

NOTES:

NOTES: